*First Ladies*

# Dolley Madison

Joanne Mattern

**ABDO**
Publishing Company

## visit us at
## www.abdopublishing.com

Published by ABDO Publishing Company, 8000 West 78th Street, Edina, Minnesota 55439.
Copyright © 2008 by Abdo Consulting Group, Inc. International copyrights reserved in all
countries. No part of this book may be reproduced in any form without written permission from the
publisher. The Checkerboard Library™ is a trademark and logo of ABDO Publishing Company.

Printed in the United States.

Cover Photo: Getty Images
Interior Photos: AP Images pp. 11, 19, 23, 24, 27; Corbis pp. 14, 21; Getty Images pp. 5, 17, 22, 25;
    Library of Congress pp. 6, 20; Macculloch Hall Historical Museum p. 15; North Wind pp. 7, 8,
    9, 10, 13, 16, 18

Series Coordinator: BreAnn Rumsch
Editors: Megan M. Gunderson, BreAnn Rumsch
Art Direction & Cover Design: Neil Klinepier

### Library of Congress Cataloging-in-Publication Data

Mattern, Joanne, 1963-
  Dolley Madison / Joanne Mattern.
    p. cm. -- (First ladies)
  Includes index.
  ISBN-13: 978-1-59928-798-0
  1. Madison, Dolley, 1768-1849--Juvenile literature. 2. Presidents' spouses--United States--
Biography--Juvenile literature. I. Title.
  E342.1.M28 2007
  973.81092--dc22
  [B]

                                                    2007009726

# Contents

# Dolley Madison

During her lifetime, Dolley Madison was one of the most famous women in the United States. She was married to James Madison, the nation's fourth president. The Madisons lived in the White House from 1809 to 1817.

President Madison adored his wife. So did the American people. Mrs. Madison loved to host parties and entertain guests. She was known as a charming hostess throughout her years in Washington, D.C.

During the **War of 1812**, Mrs. Madison rescued several national treasures from being destroyed. Her bravery led her to be regarded as a national hero.

Mrs. Madison's actions as First Lady set a strong example for future women who would fill the role. Today, she is remembered as a well respected and beloved First Lady. In fact, Mrs. Madison is considered one of the most popular First Ladies in U.S. history.

*Dolley Madison was the best-loved First Lady of the 1800s.*

# A Happy Childhood

On May 20, 1768, Dolley Payne was born in Guilford County, North Carolina. Her parents, John and Mary Coles Payne, were happy to finally have a daughter. They already had two sons. Over the next several years, the Paynes had three more daughters and two more sons.

When Dolley was less than one year old, the family moved to Hanover County, Virginia. The Paynes lived on several different plantations there. They worked hard, but they lived well.

Since Dolley was the eldest daughter, she helped her mother with housekeeping and child care. The Paynes also had slaves who helped on the farm and did housework. One slave named Mother Amy looked after the Payne children.

*When the Paynes moved to Virginia, they stayed at Scotchtown, their friend Patrick Henry's home. Mr. Henry later became the state's first governor.*

Family time was important to the Paynes. They often sat around the fireplace after dinner. There, they shared stories and sang songs. Dolley's childhood was happy. She knew that her family loved her very much.

In the 1700s, cooking took much of the day. So, Dolley's chores were an important contribution to her family.

# Life as a Quaker

The Paynes belonged to a religion called the **Society of Friends**. Members of this group are known as Quakers. John and Mary were important members of their church. They led meetings and kept records. Later, John became a Quaker preacher.

*The Payne family attended their local Quaker meetings every month.*

Quakers followed many **strict** rules. For example, they had to wear plain clothes. And, they were not allowed to play cards, dance, or attend public concerts or plays. They were only allowed to go to events put on by the Society of Friends. In addition, Quaker children were only permitted to play with other Quaker children.

However, Quakers believed that both girls and

boys should be educated. So like her brothers and sisters, Dolley attended a Quaker school. There, she learned to read and write.

Dolley enjoyed school. But, she did not like the other rules of her religion. She liked parties and pretty, colorful clothes. As Dolley grew older, she had a difficult time following the rules.

Dolley was lucky to attend school. At that time, girls usually stayed home to help with chores.

# War!

When Dolley was eight years old, the **American Revolution** began. Many battles took place in Virginia, near her home. But, the Quaker religion did not allow its members to fight in the war. So, Dolley's father and brothers did not join the military.

As the war progressed, many laws were changed. One change pleased the Paynes very much. In 1782, Virginia passed a law that said slaveholders could choose to free their slaves. So, the Paynes made a big decision. They freed all of their slaves, because owning slaves went against Quaker beliefs.

However, it soon became impossible to run the plantation without any help. So in 1783, the Paynes sold their land and moved to Philadelphia, Pennsylvania. Dolley was about to begin a new life in the big city!

*American colonists in every part of the country wanted to join the Revolution.*

Each year at Christmas, reenactors march to Washington Crossing, Pennsylvania. There, they re-create George Washington's famous crossing of the Delaware River during the American Revolution.

# A New Home

Dolley was 15 years old when her family moved to a small house in Philadelphia. There, her father started a new business selling laundry starch. Although the family was comfortable, living in a crowded city was difficult at first. Life there was very different from the country life Dolley was used to.

At the time, Philadelphia was the nation's capital. In 1783, about 40,000 people were living there. The city had schools, a large hospital, a theater, markets, and beautiful gardens. Dolley loved to watch people walking in the streets. She especially enjoyed seeing women wearing fancy gowns. Dolley wished she could dress like that, too.

Philadelphia was also home to many Quakers. So, Dolley had plenty of friends. She loved going to picnics, tea parties, meetings, and other social events.

In 1786, Dolley met a young law student named John Todd Jr. He was a Quaker, just like Dolley. John fell in love with her right away. Dolley liked spending time with John. However, she was not yet ready to get married.

During the late 1700s, Philadelphia was the second-largest U.S. city. Today, many famous buildings from Dolley's lifetime still stand.

# Hard Times

In Philadelphia, the Payne family endured some hardships. Mary gave birth to another daughter. Sadly, the baby died a few months later. Then, Dolley's older brother Walter sailed to England. The family never saw him again.

In 1789, John's business went **bankrupt**. The Quakers were angry at John for not paying his bills. So, he was banned from attending Quaker meetings. And, Mary had to take in boarders to earn money for the family.

Through these difficult times, John Todd was always by Dolley's side. In 1790, they were married in a simple Quaker ceremony. The **newlyweds** remained in Philadelphia, where John ran a successful law office.

In 1791, the couple moved into a larger home. And in February 1792, they welcomed their first child, John Payne. Dolley decided to call him Payne. She happily cared for her new family.

*Dolley enjoyed being lady of the house during her marriage to John.*

However, 1793 turned out to be a terrible year. Many people in Philadelphia became sick with **yellow fever**. Dolley and John had a second son, William Temple, in September. Tragically, John and the baby both died of the disease on October 24. Dolley was a widow at just 25 years old.

*John Todd*

## Outbreak!

For the residents of Philadelphia, Pennsylvania, 1793 was a horrible year. In the spring, the city received a lot of rain. The summer was especially hot. These conditions allowed mosquitoes to lay more eggs than normal. Then, new residents came from tropical climates, bringing yellow fever with them. Soon, the city's large mosquito population became infected and rapidly spread the disease.

The city's doctors did not know what to do! They advised healthy people to flee the city. So, many families were separated. It is estimated that between 2,000 and 4,000 people died that summer. This was equal to 10 percent of Philadelphia's population at that time.

The Philadelphia epidemic was the largest in American history. The infections finally stopped in November, when frost killed off the mosquitoes.

Today, yellow fever is rarely a problem in America. This is because the disease is prevented with a vaccine. Children receive the vaccine at a very young age. Unfortunately, many tropical parts of the world still experience yellow fever. So, it will always be important to use the vaccine.

# Meeting James

Dolley missed John very much. Thankfully, he had left her with enough money to live comfortably. Dolley and her son Payne stayed in Philadelphia. Soon, Dolley's 14-year-old sister, Anna, moved in with them. Slowly, life returned to normal.

Dolley had many friends who were important members of the government. One of them was a man named Aaron Burr. One day, Aaron introduced Dolley to his friend James Madison.

Dolley enjoyed meeting James. He was 17 years older than she was. James was also a wealthy, well-educated

*Many people called James "the Great Little Madison." This is because he was only 66 inches (168 cm) tall.*

16

congressman from Virginia. He had helped write the U.S. **Constitution** and the **Bill of Rights**. James liked Dolley very much. But, he was shy. So, he wrote Dolley many letters.

Soon, James asked Dolley to marry him. Everyone in Philadelphia was talking about the couple and their romance. On September 15, 1794, Dolley and James were happily married.

*Dolley had her portrait painted just weeks after she and James wed.*

# A Political Wife

Mr. Madison was not a Quaker. So after they married, Mrs. Madison had to leave the **Society of Friends**. She did not really mind. She no longer had to follow **strict** rules about plain dress. Now she could wear the fashionable, pretty clothes she loved.

In 1800, Washington, D.C., became the capital of the United States. That same year, Thomas Jefferson was elected the third U.S. president. He named Mr. Madison the **secretary of state**. This was an important government position. The Madisons moved to Washington, D.C., in May 1801.

President Jefferson also needed a hostess for political gatherings. His wife had died many years earlier. So, he asked Mrs. Madison for her help. Since she loved giving parties, she was happy to agree.

*Thomas Jefferson was a good friend to the Madisons.*

Mrs. Madison invited many different people to the president's parties. Sometimes, these people disagreed over political issues. But when they argued, Mrs. Madison quickly changed the subject so her guests would not fight. She had a talent for putting people at ease. Soon, she was the most popular woman in Washington.

*Mrs. Madison's charm and sense of humor made her guests feel warmly welcomed.*

# A New Sense of Style

The Madisons remained important in Washington throughout President Jefferson's term. On March 4, 1809, Mr. Madison became the fourth president of the United States. Americans were glad Mrs. Madison was the new First Lady. People liked and admired her for many reasons. She respected different opinions on political issues and treated everyone equally. And, she was very proud of her country.

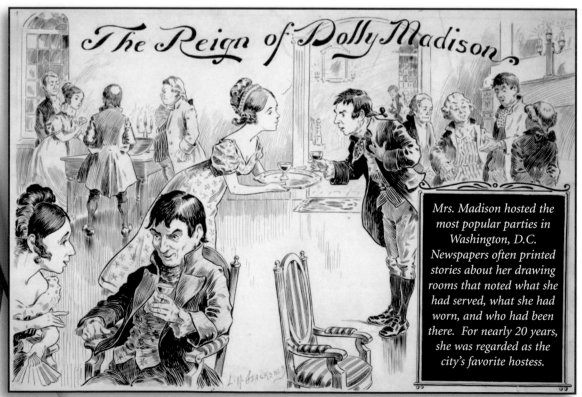

*The Reign of Dolly Madison*

*Mrs. Madison hosted the most popular parties in Washington, D.C. Newspapers often printed stories about her drawing rooms that noted what she had served, what she had worn, and who had been there. For nearly 20 years, she was regarded as the city's favorite hostess.*

Many people looked to the president and his home for ideas about entertaining. The First Lady hosted parties, government dinners, and other events. She welcomed guests almost every night. Usually, she entertained government officials and other important figures.

But on Wednesdays, Mrs. Madison opened her parties to the public. These gatherings were called "drawing rooms." The First Lady made each guest feel welcome. And, everyone was treated with respect.

Mrs. Madison also helped decorate the President's House. Later, this building would be called the White House. The First Lady was more stylish than anyone! She loved to wear fancy gowns, gloves, slippers, hats, and jewelry. Some people said Mrs. Madison dressed like a queen.

# The British are Coming!

Shortly before President Madison was reelected in 1812, the United States entered a difficult time. The country became involved in the **War of 1812**, a conflict with Great Britain. On August 19, 1814, British soldiers marched toward Washington, D.C. By August 24, the president had decided to meet with the U.S. army.

Mrs. Madison and a few others stayed at the President's House. But later that day, she heard British cannons firing on the city. The First Lady did not want important government papers to fall into British hands. So she acted quickly. She packed many papers and other belongings into a wagon and left the capital city.

*The First Lady's courage saved many national treasures from the flames.*

British soldiers reached the President's House soon after Mrs. Madison had left. In fact, they sat down to the hot meal she had prepared for her husband! After their dinner, the soldiers burned the house and many other government buildings.

*Stuart's portrait contains meaningful symbols about America.*

## A National Hero

Mrs. Madison is the only First Lady who has had to face an invasion of the White House! However, she handled the crisis with quick thinking. Mrs. Madison packed as many treasures as she could. She made sure to rescue her husband's papers and a copy of the Declaration of Independence. She also took some curtains and the blue and gold set of china she had purchased for state dinners.

Mrs. Madison especially wanted to rescue a large painting of George Washington. Hurriedly, she had her servants break the frame, pull out the painting, and roll it up. Mrs. Madison left the city by carriage, just minutes before the British troops arrived.

The portrait of George Washington was painted by Gilbert Stuart, an important American artist. He created four similar paintings, known today as the Lansdowne portraits. Without Mrs. Madison's fast thinking, the painting would most likely have been destroyed in the fire.

Today, the painting is well protected by the Smithsonian Institute, one of America's most important museums. The painting represents important ideas about the United States at the time it was painted. It remains one of the nation's oldest and most valued treasures.

# Alone Once More

After the British soldiers left Washington, D.C., the Madisons returned to the capital. However, they had to stay in a friend's home while the President's House was rebuilt.

On December 24, 1814, the United States and Great Britain signed the Treaty of Ghent. This ended the **War of 1812**. For the next two years, President Madison and other politicians rebuilt

*Montpelier was surrounded by hills and filled with beautiful flower gardens.*

Washington, D.C. Mrs. Madison kept their spirits up by hosting parties and drawing rooms.

On March 4, 1817, President Madison finished his second term in office. The Madisons retired to Montpelier, their plantation near Richmond, Virginia. Mr. Madison spent most days writing letters. Mrs. Madison helped him organize his political papers. In the evenings, they entertained guests and hosted many dinner parties.

Mr. and Mrs. Madison loved each other very much.

*Mrs. Madison remained connected to friends in Washington, D.C., during her husband's retirement.*

Mrs. Madison once wrote, "Our hearts understand each other." As the years passed, her husband's health began to fail. Sadly, Mr. Madison died at Montpelier on June 28, 1836. Mrs. Madison was a widow for the second time. She was comforted by the many letters she received.

# A Life Remembered

After her husband died, Mrs. Madison wanted to publish his presidential papers. In April 1837, Congress bought some of the papers and published them. Soon after, Mrs. Madison returned to Washington, D.C., where many of her friends still lived. She began attending parties and dinners again.

Still, Mrs. Madison often visited Montpelier. She had trusted her son Payne to run the plantation. Unfortunately, he did such a poor job that she was forced to sell the estate in 1844. Later, Congress published the rest of Mr. Madison's papers. This raised enough money for Mrs. Madison to live comfortably in Washington, D.C., for the rest of her life.

By summer 1849, Mrs. Madison's health was poor. She died at home on July 12, surrounded by friends and family. Thousands of people mourned her death. Her funeral procession was the largest the city had ever seen. As a special honor, Mrs. Madison was buried in the Congressional Cemetery. However, her body was later moved to the cemetery at Montpelier.

Dolley Madison's spirit, grace, and charm have been remembered long after her death. Today, she remains one of America's most popular and famous First Ladies. Mrs. Madison will always be remembered for changing the role of First Lady. She became an example of how a First Lady can support her husband, as well as her country and its people.

*Though she was First Lady for only eight years, Mrs. Madison was recognized as an important political figure for more than 50 years.*

# Timeline

| | |
|---|---|
| 1768 | Dolley Payne was born on May 20. |
| 1783 | Dolley's family moved to Philadelphia, Pennsylvania. |
| 1790 | Dolley married John Todd Jr. |
| 1792 | Dolley and John's son John Payne was born in February. |
| 1793 | Dolley and John's son William Temple was born in September; on October 24, John and baby William both died of yellow fever. |
| 1794 | Dolley married James Madison on September 15. |
| 1801 | Mr. Madison became secretary of state; the Madisons moved to Washington, D.C.; Mrs. Madison began acting as President Jefferson's official hostess. |
| 1809–1817 | Mrs. Madison acted as First Lady, while her husband served as president. |
| 1814 | Mrs. Madison rescued important documents and national treasures from the President's House on August 24. |
| 1836 | Mr. Madison died on June 28. |
| 1837 | Mrs. Madison sold some of her husband's presidential papers to Congress to be published. |
| 1849 | Mrs. Madison died on July 12. |

# Did You Know?

Though her parents recorded her name at birth, Dolley has mistakenly been called Dolly, as well as Dorothy or Dorthea, throughout the years.

Due to her popularity as a hostess, many food companies have used Dolley Madison's name to sell their products, such as ice cream, cookies, popcorn, and doughnuts.

Mrs. Madison was the first First Lady to attend a presidential inauguration in Washington, D.C.

Mrs. Madison was the first woman to redecorate the White House.

In 1812, Mrs. Madison made the arrangements for the first wedding held at the White House.  There, her sister Lucy married Supreme Court Justice Thomas Todd.

Mrs. Madison purchased the White House's first piano and first collection of music.  Unfortunately, these items were destroyed in the 1814 fire.

Mrs. Madison owned a green parrot named Polly.

After Mr. Madison died, Congress granted Mrs. Madison a lifetime seat on the floor of the House of Representatives.  This was the highest honor ever given to a president's widow.

# Glossary

**American Revolution** - from 1775 to 1783. A war for independence between Great Britain and its North American colonies. The colonists won and created the United States of America.

**bankrupt** - legally declared unable to pay debts.

**Bill of Rights** - a summary of rights in the U.S. Constitution that the United States guarantees to the American people.

**Constitution** - the laws that govern the United States.

**newlywed** - a person who just married.

**secretary of state** - a member of the president's cabinet who handles relations with other countries.

**Society of Friends** - a Christian group first developed in England during the 1600s, in opposition to the Catholic Church. Followers reject worldly goods and honors, believing instead that all people are equal to receive the word of God.

**strict** - demanding others to follow rules or regulations in a rigid, exact manner.

**War of 1812** - from 1812 to 1814.  A war fought between the United States and Great Britain over shipping rights and the capture of U.S. soldiers.

**yellow fever** - a disease transmitted by the yellow-fever mosquito, usually in warm climates.  It is marked by fever, headache, yellow-colored skin, and internal bleeding.

# Web Sites

To learn more about Dolley Madison, visit ABDO Publishing Company on the World Wide Web at **www.abdopublishing.com**. Web sites about Dolley Madison are featured on our Book Links page.  These links are routinely monitored and updated to provide the most current information available.

# Index